Religion. and the Constitution

John Charles Daly, moderator

Walter Berns
Edd Doerr
Henry J. Hyde
Barry William Lynn

Held on May 22, 1984
and sponsored by
the American Enterprise Institute
for Public Policy Research
Washington and London

The AEI Project, "A Decade of Study of the Constitution," of which publication of this Public Policy Forum transcript is one activity, has been funded in part by a grant from the National Endowment for the Humanities.

Distributed to the Trade by National Book Network, 15200 NBN Way, Blue Ridge Summit, PA 17214. To order call toll free 1-800-462-6420 or 1-717-794-3800. For all other inquiries please contact the AEI Press, 1150 Seventeenth Street, N.W., Washington, D.C. 20036 or call 1-800-862-5801.

This pamphlet contains the edited transcript
of one of a series of AEI forums.
These forums offer a medium for
informal exchanges of ideas on current policy problems
of national and international import.
As part of AEI's program of providing opportunities
for the presentation of competing views,
they serve to enhance the prospect
that decisions within our democracy will be based
on a more informed public opinion.
AEI forums are also available on
audio and color-video cassettes.

AEI Forum 62

ISBN 0–8447–2249–9
Library of Congress Catalog Card No. 84–71858

JOHN CHARLES DALY, former ABC News chief: This public policy forum, one of a series presented by the American Enterprise Institute, examines the relationship of church and state under the Constitution of the United States. Our subject: religion and the Constitution.

Our Constitution, hammered out in the long debate in Philadelphia in 1787, went to the states for ratification bearing one reference to religion. Article VI states: "No religious Test shall ever be required as a Qualification to any Office or public Trust under the United States."

After months of debate in the states, the Constitution was ratified. The states made it clear, however, that the First Congress was expected to act immediately on amendments protecting specific rights, among them religious rights. In its first sitting then, the Congress debated and passed, and the states subsequently ratified, ten amendments—our Bill of Rights.

The First Amendment declares, in part: "Congress shall make no law respecting an establishment of religion"—this is known as the Establishment Clause—"or prohibiting the free exercise thereof"—this is known as the Free Exercise Clause.

This brief, albeit comprehensive, declaration of religious rights was distilled from a familiar background. The thirteen colonies were settled substantially by families fleeing religious persecution in England and elsewhere in Europe, and religion was a dominant factor in the colonies where, by the way, religious persecution was not entirely unknown.

At the time of our Revolution, nine of the thirteen colonies still had established religions—the Puritan Congregational church in Massachusetts, New Hampshire, and Connecticut, and the Anglican church in New York, Maryland, Virginia, North and South Carolina, and Georgia. Moreover, five states had established religions as the First Amendment was drafted, and restrictions of one kind or another affecting some religious beliefs existed in five other states.

1

The two clauses, the Establishment Clause and the Free Exercise Clause, have been intensely debated as to their scope and meaning and the original intent of the founders concerning them. In modern times, that intensity of debate increased markedly in 1947, with the Supreme Court decision in *Everson* v. *Board of Education*. In its opinion, the Court held that the Establishment Clause was made wholly applicable to the states by the Fourteenth Amendment's Due Process Clause, and over time the application of both the Establishment and the Free Exercise clauses to the states through the Fourteenth Amendment played a major role in other cases before the Supreme Court. There were cases involving Sunday closing laws and the right to unemployment benefits when a religiously mandated Saturday non-workday made many jobs unavailable. In Wisconsin, there was the refusal on religious grounds by members of the Old Order Amish to send their children to school past the eighth grade; in Maryland, a commission was denied to a notary public because the candidate would not declare a belief in God; in Tennessee, a law prohibited ministers from serving in the legislature or serving as delegates to the Constitutional Convention; all were issues that came before the Court.

In very recent times, on the legislative front, proposed amendments have been defeated in the Senate concerning voluntary vocal and silent prayer. The Congress rejected and then passed an "equal access" bill, designed to ensure that student religious groups in public high schools have the same rights as secular student clubs to meet on school grounds. Church groups, by the way, were divided on that bill, and civil liberties experts, who normally agree on almost all sensitive legislation of this kind, also were in disagreement.

There are other issues that seem pressing to various constituencies: teaching creationism in science education; the Supreme Court's recent crèche decision, affirming the constitutionality of including religious symbols in holiday displays on public grounds; and issues such as conscientious objector status in military registration, and the naming of an official ambassador to the Vatican.

To guide us through this complex and contentious relationship between the Constitution and religion, we have an expert panel. Mr. Walter Berns is John M. Olin Distinguished Scholar in Constitutional and Legal Studies at the American Enterprise Institute and the author of *The First Amendment and the Future of American Democracy*. Representative Henry J. Hyde, Republican member of the House of Representatives from Illinois, is serving his fifth term. Representative Hyde is a member of the House Judiciary Committee and serves on the Subcommittee on Courts, Civil Liberties, and the Administration of Justice. Mr. Edd Doerr is executive director of Americans for Religious Liberty, and former editor of *Church and State* magazine. And the Reverend Barry Lynn is legislative counsel in the Washington office of the American Civil Liberties Union. He has been legislative counsel in the Office for Church in Society, United Church of Christ and is also an ordained minister of the United Church of Christ.

To begin, gentlemen, I would pose the same question to each of you in turn. Does government have an obligation to support religion as one way of helping to sustain a free society? Our nation's motto is "In God We Trust." The president, members of Congress, judges, and other public servants often swear their oaths of office on the Bible. Each day of the congressional session begins with a prayer for guidance. Should government help strengthen religious values in other ways?

HENRY J. HYDE, U.S. representative (Republican, Illinois): I think government may do so within the confines of the Constitution, as long as it does not prefer one sect or religious group over another. The hostility toward all religion that seems to be the result of the *Everson* case was never before true. We have had government support for chaplains, not only in the military, but in the House and Senate, and James Madison was on the committee that provided for them. We always have had relationships of a sort between religious groups and government, but the Constitution requires that they be such as not to set up a state religion, a national religion, and, certainly, not to prefer one religion over another.

EDD DOERR, executive director, Americans for Religious Liberty: The best thing that the state can do for religion is to keep its hands off it, to let religion stay in the private sector. Government should not force citizens involuntarily, through taxation, to support religion. Government should not meddle with the religious lives of children or adults. It should not discriminate in any way for or against various churches. Unfortunately, though our history for two centuries since the adoption of the Constitution has been one of reaffirming and furthering the separation of church and state that Jefferson and Madison spoke so highly of, in the last few years we have seen tremendous efforts toward the piecemeal repeal of the First Amendment. There are efforts in state capitals and in Congress to tax people for the support of religious institutions, efforts to amend the Constitution to authorize civil servants to meddle with children's religious lives, and efforts by government to interfere with the conscience rights of women to determine whether or not they will become mothers. The president recently extended diplomatic relations to a single church to the exclusion of all others. These are some of the examples of how government has been moving away from the neutrality toward religion that is required by the Constitution.

WALTER BERNS, John M. Olin Distinguished Scholar in Constitutional and Legal Studies, American Enterprise Institute: Mr. Daly, in your question you used the word "obligation," that is, does the government have an obligation to support religious values? Strictly speaking, of course, the government has no obligation in the sense that it has a constitutional obligation, as stated in Article IV of the Constitution, to guarantee a republican form of government to each of the states. So the question really is not whether the government has an obligation, but whether it would be well advised to support religion, or whether there are some compelling reasons why it should. I agree with Mr. Doerr that, of course, the purpose of the First Amendment is to subordinate religion to the private sphere. The question then becomes whether the government is *forbidden* by the First Amendment to provide assistance to religion in the private sphere and to act in one way or another to see to it that religion in the private sphere maintains its vitality. The answer to that question probably turns on whether it is understood by us, as it was understood by Americans in the beginning, that there is some connection between the sort of moral training that the churches provide and a healthy, liberal democracy in the United States. That, I think, is the way the issue should be phrased.

BARRY W. LYNN, legislative counsel, American Civil Liberties Union: It is important that we recognize not only that the government may not be hostile to religion, but that it must be very strictly neutral regarding religion. This means at least several things. First, it means the government must preserve the right of conscience for all Americans, so that persons are not forced to support religious practices with which they disagree. Second, it means that the government must scrupulously avoid involvement in religious matters and may not supervise religious institutions. Third, neutrality means the government must not create political warfare over sectarian religious matters. And, finally, government neutrality regarding religion is necessary so as not to degrade the practice of religion itself.

The question for this decade and the decades to come is not so much what the framers may have thought about the Constitution nearly 200 years ago, but how those majestic generalities in the First Amendment are to be construed today as concrete restraints on what the government can do.

4

MR. BERNS: In other words, the Constitution changes its meaning over time?

MR. LYNN: I think the Constitution is a living document; it must remain such. In fact, it is very interesting that Mr. Hyde mentioned that James Madison voted for the establishment of congressional chaplains. It is important to mention that several years later as president, he wrote a document opposing the continuation of the practice of having congressional chaplains because he felt it was a First Amendment violation. Even if not at the beginning, by the time he was president I am sure he would have fit very well in the American Civil Liberties Union.

MR. BERNS: Yes, but the issue is whether the Constitution changes its meaning over time and, apparently, your answer to that is, "Yes, indeed, it does change its meaning over time." So what controls the direction in which the Constitution moves?

MR. LYNN: The way in which, and the circumstances under which, one delicately balances the requirements of the Free Exercise Clause with the guarantee that there shall be no establishment of religion. There is a tension between the religion clauses, whether or not the framers of the Constitution initially recognized it. To call it a tension is perhaps too polite. In some ways there is a contradiction between those two clauses, and to the maximum extent possible, we must guarantee the right of conscience and the right of free exercise, so that persons may exercise their consciences in complete accord with their religious beliefs.

REPRESENTATIVE HYDE: I agree with everything you have said, Mr. Lynn, but much more important and fundamental is the question Mr. Berns raised: How does this "living" document change, and how do we learn what its changes mean? Now, if an unelected group of nine people on the bench of the Supreme Court, through some insight— or, as Justice Jackson said in his concurring opinion in *Everson*, through "no law but our own prepossession"—is going to determine what this document means today, rather than the legislative branch, which is accountable, electable, and recallable by the people, then we have gotten away from the consent of the governed and are back to the divine right of kings.

MR. LYNN: By creating this dichotomy, one creates the possibility that majority rule, as reflected by members of Congress and their constituents, will be the arbiter, the final arbiter, of constitutional values. It has been clear since *Marbury* vs. *Madison* that in fact it is the Supreme Court that is the arbiter, finally, of what the First Amendment and the rest of the Constitution means, and that is the way it should be.

REPRESENTATIVE HYDE: Yes, but I would suggest that the task of the Court is to adjudicate, and not to legislate, not to find things in the Constitution that are not there, that never were contemplated by the framers. The framers, in their wisdom, provided a way to amend the Constitution, but they made it tough. They required an extraordinary majority in the House and in the Senate for passage of an amendment, and thirty-eight states to ratify. That is tough. But they did not say that a majority of five men or women on the Court can change the Constitution. They said, "Go out to the people and change it." That is what we have gotten away from.

MR. DOERR: Whether the Court changes the Constitution is a matter of opinion, but the Constitution was written 200 years ago, and the founders are long since dead. When there is an apparent conflict over constitutional rights, the Supreme Court does not exactly legislate, but it settles disputes between parties, between those who go into court with a real controversy. Both parties make constitutional claims, and the Supreme Court and the lower federal courts have to decide who has the better claim.

It is stretching things to say that the Court is legislating. The justices are the guardians of the Constitution, and without them, Congress could run roughshod over our liberties, as it has sometimes done in the heat of passion.

MR. BERNS: The question is, Are they guardians of a Constitution that has a relatively fixed meaning, or are they guardians of something that they themselves create? If they are the guardians of something that they themselves create, there is no problem here at all, because they will guard it as a father guards his child, and the miser his money.

MR. DOERR: What is your solution to that?

MR. BERNS: Solution to what? I just keep asking whether the Constitution changes its meaning; perhaps we have to settle that before we go any further.

MR. LYNN: It is also important to realize that most of what was in the minds of the people in the Congress that sent the Bill of Rights out to

6

the states and certainly most of what was in the minds of the state legislators who ratified the Bill of Rights is totally unknown information. It is not possible for us to go back and seek the original intention.

MR. BERNS: That is not so. We know what went on in the Congress. We know what James Madison said in the First Congress in 1789. We know what Samuel Livermore said with respect to this.

MR. LYNN: Well, they were not the only people voting on the matter.

REPRESENTATIVE HYDE: The day after the First Amendment was adopted by Congress, the Congress petitioned the president to issue a proclamation for prayer and thanksgiving. For anybody to say that Congress within twenty-four hours reversed itself and adopted a policy of hostility toward religion—the "wall of separation" that Justice Black erected in 1947—is unhistorical.

MR. LYNN: It is also not clear that the members of Congress 200 years ago fully recognized the implications of everything they did. That is why they sometimes spoke in general terms.

REPRESENTATIVE HYDE: You mean they did not know what they were doing in the First Congress? The first thing they did was to get a chaplain. They have opened their sessions every day, including today, with a prayer, as does the Supreme Court.

MR. DOERR: How many people were there in congressional session when the prayer was read this morning?

REPRESENTATIVE HYDE: On closed-circuit television? I would say 90 percent.

MR. DOERR: It is a pro forma thing, actually. If you read the history—

REPRESENTATIVE HYDE: Then it does not count? Is that what you mean?

MR. DOERR: Reading the history of the period of the Constitutional Convention, the Washington administration, and the Congresses of that time reveals that there was just as much conflict in politics then as now. Even the greatest men in the United States were inconsistent. Madison, Jefferson, and Washington all committed inconsistencies.

MR. BERNS: And what follows from that? I don't understand.

MR. DOERR: What follows from that is our recognition that they were human. They could not have foreseen all of the problems that would come up under the Bill of Rights. But, under our living Constitution, we have had the longest-running constitutional government in history, and it works pretty well.

MR. BERNS: Hear! Hear! And the Constitution says the president has to be thirty-five years of age. Now, does the living quality of the Constitution indicate that, in time, thirty-five will mean something other than thirty-five?

MR. LYNN: Very little is necessary to interpret the meaning of "thirty-five years of age." There is a great deal of interpretation necessary, however, when we are talking about the free exercise of religion or the guarantee of no establishment of religion. That is what the Supreme Court is designed to do and is capable of doing; whether or not you or I agree with all of its decisions, that body of people is vested with the power to make those decisions.

MR. BERNS: Well, Mr. Lynn, unless we agree that these words in the First Amendment mean something, our discussion here today will be your opinion about the Constitution versus my opinion about the Constitution, and neither opinion is to be preferred to the other. We have to agree that these words mean something. Of course they are more ambiguous than "thirty-five years of age," and more ambiguous than "states shall not issue letters of marque," a phrase so unambiguous that no state has ever issued a letter of marque. These words, however, do mean something.

I agree that the two parts of the First Amendment having to do with religion contradict each other when carried to the extreme. Nevertheless, one can learn something from those words; one can learn something from what the members of the First Congress said with respect to them; one can learn something from what James Madison said; one can learn something from the political philosophy that informed this amendment. But the words have to *mean* something, or we are just uttering opinions here.

MR. DOERR: But one can conclude from the deliberations of the 1780s and 1790s that a civil religion of sorts was in vogue. Men who were not orthodox Christians —for instance, Jefferson and Washington—made invocations to the Deity. But these were rather ceremonial examples of a civil religion that was in vogue at the time.

REPRESENTATIVE HYDE: What do you mean by a "civil religion"? There is a recognition of the fatherhood of God and the omnipotence of the Supreme Being in the Thanksgiving proclamations of Washington, his Farewell Address, and the Northwest Ordinance, where federal money was provided for churches and schools and for teaching the Indians. Our Founding Fathers were very concerned about the Indians. They provided money for priests and for churches so that the Indians could be taught Christianity and this took place closer to the time of the drafting of that First Amendment.

I am not disagreeing with the wisdom of what you are saying, but we are talking about what the Constitution means, what the framers understood it to mean, and who should say what it means today.

MR. DOERR: Madison, for example, was one of the primary architects of the Bill of Rights; as president he vetoed legislation passed by Congress that would have granted $10 worth of land in the Mississippi Territory to a Baptist church. His veto message makes clear that it was this sort of thing that the First Amendment was written to prohibit.

MR. BERNS: The ambiguity of this is, I think, reflected in the fact that what you have said is absolutely correct, and what I am about to say is also absolutely correct.

Here is Article III of the Northwest Ordinance that Representative Hyde referred to and that was adopted by the First Congress of the United States, the same Congress that proposed the First Amendment. And James Madison voted for this: "Religion, morality, and knowledge being necessary to good government and the happiness of mankind, schools and the means of learning shall forever be encouraged."

MR. DOERR: Was that not passed in 1787?

MR. BERNS: It was, of course, originally passed by the Continental Congress in 1787, but it was immediately readopted to give it strength under the new Constitution—"readopted" is, I think, the exact phrase used by the First Congress of the United States. You see, the question I posed originally is this, and I think this is a fair statement of it: Do we agree or disagree that religion, morality, and knowledge are necessary to good government? If they are, then it might follow, and the First Amendment might have room for, a program of assistance on a non-discriminatory basis, across-the-board, to all churches, all religions, all sects. That is my position, and I suspect it is Congressman Hyde's position.

9

REPRESENTATIVE HYDE: As late as 1896, Congress was appropriating $500,000 for religious education of the Indians. The Supreme Court never bit into the Establishment Clause until 1947, in the *Everson* case.

MR. DOERR: Were they not treaty-governed funds that belonged to the Indians in the first place, and did the Supreme Court not find, in the 1890s, I believe, that since they were Indian funds, the federal government was merely administering them in accordance with the wishes of the Indians?

REPRESENTATIVE HYDE: No. Congress changed the policy in 1897. Until then, the policy had been to provide the churches with funds.

There is a whole litany of treaties—made by Thomas Jefferson, Andrew Jackson, Martin Van Buren, John Quincy Adams—and all were signed to provide funds for building churches and to provide salaries for clergymen to Christianize the Indians. There was a great reason for that at the time.

MR. DOERR: But they were able to stay away from spending any money to Christianize whites. They stayed away from that.

REPRESENTATIVE HYDE: Well, they had chaplains to do that in Congress—where we needed the prayers everyday—and in the military.

MR. DALY: I mentioned earlier that the Senate defeated proposed amendments to the Constitution relating to voluntary prayer, both vocal and silent, in public schools. Neither was passed in the Senate, in spite of strong evidence in public opinion polls that a large majority of Americans favor some form of voluntary prayer in public schools. Should public polling play a paramount part in congressional and court decisions on religious issues?

MR. LYNN: No, it absolutely should not, though that was one of the principal arguments used by those who would amend the Constitution. It was not an argument for what is *truly* voluntary prayer, however, because truly voluntary prayer is permitted in public schools now. No state school board official is going to come into a school lunchroom and try to stop someone from saying grace before he or she has lunch. No one is going to try to stop a basketball player from crossing himself before he takes the foul shot.

What the Senate was attempting to do was to prescribe that a minute be set aside at the beginning of each school day for the states to permit state-selected—not necessarily state-written, but state-selected—

prayer, which would be sectarian prayer, which would be the establishment of religion, and which would be in very serious conflict, not just with the Establishment Clause as it exists today, but with the very notion of government neutrality in regard to religion.

REPRESENTATIVE HYDE: I have trouble being told about some particular religious philosophy being thrust on anybody, especially with the discipline that a school structure has. By the same token, it seems incongruous that state legislatures and the federal Congress open every day with a prayer prescribed by somebody. I have never been asked for my selection by the chaplain who is paid with tax dollars; the Supreme Court says "God save the Constitution and this Court"; oaths are taken on Bibles. Everybody can pray one way or another in a structured manner except the kid in school. And I have problems with that.

MR. DOERR: When the Congress prays in the morning, they all do not stand up and recite the same prayer. Every member of Congress does not do this.

REPRESENTATIVE HYDE: We usually bow our heads and listen.

MR. DOERR: In your own state of Illinois, Mr. Hyde, school prayer was done away with before any of us were born and the citizens of Illinois who have grown up since 1900 don't seem to be any the worse for it.

REPRESENTATIVE HYDE: We have some problems in Illinois —in Chicago. I will take you for a walk some evening and we will both pray we get out of the neighborhood. [Laughter.]

MR. LYNN: Let's do it on the streets, not in the schools.

REPRESENTATIVE HYDE: Let's do it both places.

MR. LYNN: Silent prayer is another issue that means a great deal more than it might seem at first blush. There was an effort made to pass a silent prayer amendment to the Constitution that would have mandated essentially a moment of silent religious activity during the day, and the very selection of that mode of prayer is a dramatic step for any government to take.

Many people, of course, are offended by silent prayer. In fact, some of my more fundamentalist Christian friends believe that it is absolutely blasphemous to participate in silent prayer because prayer, in their

11

tradition, must be oral for it to have any meaning. So the mere distinction between silent and vocal prayer has great theological significance and certainly is not something that the Congress ought to deliberate.

REPRESENTATIVE HYDE: I am thinking of introducing a bill to have young people in school pull out the old Declaration of Independence and read the part that states, "We hold these truths to be self-evident that all men are . . . endowed by their Creator with certain unalienable Rights." I think it would be therapeutic, if not instructive, for students to cogitate on what our very Founding Fathers, way before the Constitution, had in mind.

MR. DOERR: Every child may do this now—

REPRESENTATIVE HYDE: I understand that.

MR. DOERR: —in a public school.

REPRESENTATIVE HYDE: It is not done, and I think it ought to be done. You would not object to that, would you, Mr. Doerr, to the Declaration of Independence being read in school?

MR. DOERR: I would not object to an individual child reading the Bible or the Koran in school—

REPRESENTATIVE HYDE: How about the whole class? How about the teacher saying, "Now, students, we will take out our well-worn, thumbed copy of the Declaration of Independence, and we will read it." Would you object to that?

MR. DOERR: If they do it every day for the purpose of having a religious exercise, it is objectionable, and it is trivializing the Declaration of Independence. It is degrading it.

REPRESENTATIVE HYDE: I think throwing it in the drawer and never reading it has trivialized it.

MR. DALY: Let me, if I may, come to the point of what has happened. If the facts are straight, there was evident in public polls a desire on the part of a great number of the public for voluntary vocal or silent prayer in public schools. It having been ordered by the Supreme Court that this was unconstitutional, the issue went to the Congress of the

United States, where the power is vested for proposing changes to the Constitution, and it failed.

Now, does this not say that the American process worked perfectly here? There was deep consideration by the Congress, and the Congress did not overturn the ruling by the Supreme Court. But the ability to do so is there.

MR. LYNN: It is there, and in two-and-a-half weeks of debate over the school prayer amendment, the Senate, in one of its finest hours recently, was able to defeat the amendment and decide to keep separation of church and state precisely where it is today.

REPRESENTATIVE HYDE: I agree with Mr. Lynn that the process really worked, and I think that is what our Founding Fathers intended. When you are going to change the Constitution, there is a formal and difficult process to go through. I would not say the right or the wisest result was obtained, but it was the democratic result. It was the way our Founding Fathers wanted it done, and I am proud of it in that sense.

But I would rather have that happen than have some judges decide, as Justice Jackson said, simply according to their prepossessions.

MR. DALY: Now, let's turn to the equal access issue that was before the Congress. This was the bill to guarantee access of student religious groups to school buildings on an equal basis with other student groups.

MR. BERNS: What interests me about that is the lack of public discussion as to the constitutional authority for the national government to decide whether the school system or the schools of, say, Ottumwa, Iowa, should or should not admit certain groups and give them access to school facilities to conduct their meetings. We have gone so far in this country that it is no longer a matter of discussion that the national government is assumed to have the authority to dictate that to Ottumwa. That is astonishing really.

Now, of course, the authority here in fact is tied to the federal government's giving out money; if one has the power to give money and promises or threatens to withhold it, one can do practically anything under this Constitution, and that raises problems.

As to the access question itself, what interests me is that the Supreme Court decided that religious groups could not have equal access to the use of school buildings, but if the Communist party wanted access and the schools refused that access, the Court would rule in favor of the Communist party. Conclusion: Communists may have use of our public facilities; religious groups may not. That, I think, probably was not intended by James Madison.

MR. DOERR: You're right, Mr. Berns, that it is highhanded of Congress to dictate policy to the school board in Ottumwa, Iowa, but the real issue is the gross abuse that could creep in or that would plainly be there.

There was nothing in that bill to prevent the proselytizing of children as young as eleven or twelve years, in the seventh grade, by outside adult missionaries. This sort of thing happens in many public schools. There was no safeguard against that in the bill. The sponsor of the bill had no interest in an amendment to the bill to provide these safeguards.

REPRESENTATIVE HYDE: My instinct was to support the equal access bill based on a libertarian theory that a school is a public building, paid for by public funds, and that it ought to be available to the public in an orderly fashion without chaos, so long as it is made available without discrimination.

So if the Moonies and the Hare Krishna want to come in, they are as entitled to exercise free speech as you or I, much as I would disagree with what they would say. But I do not see how we can shut the door to one group and not to another or shut the door to all groups under our Constitution.

MR. LYNN: This is a much more radical approach to religion in the public schools than even a moment of prayer, because it allows religious services; it allows doctrinal instruction as well as efforts to convert students right in the corridors and the classrooms of America's public schools.

MR. DALY: Can we discuss this in light of the fact that the Court has held that, at the public university level, equal access must be given to all groups if access is given to some. What is the great difference between this procedure now practiced in our universities and what is proposed in the public high schools?

MR. DOERR: There has to be a dividing line between people who are old enough not to be easily indoctrinated and people who are young and immature. We have age requirements for acquiring a driver's license, for consuming alcohol, for getting married—

REPRESENTATIVE HYDE: And for learning about God, is that it?

MR. DOERR: We have institutions for learning about God. They are called churches and synagogues. The Supreme Court itself has said that the public schools may offer objective academic instruction about religion, and there is much of it going on that is perfectly respectable in our public schools.

REPRESENTATIVE HYDE: You require a level of maturity, then, before these ideas about religion may be foisted on young minds?

MR. DOERR: No. We draw lines. We will not even, for instance, let children into school until they are a certain age.

REPRESENTATIVE HYDE: Sex education for the little ones is okay, but not prayer.

MR. LYNN: There is one very important distinction that also makes a difference between the case of the University of Missouri and a junior high school in Illinois, and that is that the university was an open forum. It was truly open to every known organization.

REPRESENTATIVE HYDE: Equal access, in other words?

MR. LYNN: Equal access was truly there. And in America's public schools today, it is just as difficult—in fact, I would submit it's more difficult—to get a club to study Karl Marx than it is to get a club to study the Bible.

REPRESENTATIVE HYDE: I really would think the American Civil Liberties Union would be pushing for equal access, even though there are ideas we do not agree with. Your proudest moment was also your toughest moment, and that was defending the right of the Nazis to march in public. I would not have done that. I think it would have caused a riot and, therefore, would be too inflammatory. But that took guts.

MR. LYNN: Again, in a public forum, such as a public park, we support it, but for the same reasons that we do not want religious worship services to occur in school, we do not want the Hitler youth movement to meet in school during school hours, because that would put the state's imprimatur or blessing on racially discriminatory activity in violation of the Constitution.

MR. DALY: Representative Hyde, tuition tax credits is an area of your particular interest. The issue is this: Some parents have decided that their children would receive a better education, perhaps including a deeper religious education, in private schools, both religious and non-religious, but these parents would bear two burdens: tuition for private school and taxes for public schools. They argue that it is perfectly reasonable that there should be some kind of tuition tax credit. Would you speak to this issue?

REPRESENTATIVE HYDE: Ever since 1925, the Supreme Court has held that sending one's child to a parochial school fulfills the secular requirement of a public education, a good education, because the local board of education has certified that the child is getting a decent education.

If one can fulfill the state law requirement by sending one's child to a parochial school, I do not see the constitutional difficulty—we can argue the wisdom, though that is really another question, but I am prepared to argue that too—in providing tuition tax credits. This really says to the parent, you do not have to bear this double burden; we will let you keep some of your own money because your child is going to parochial school rather than public school.

It has been held by the Court that the money you put in the collection box on Sunday does not establish a religion. That has been held by the courts. I should not think tuition tax credits would establish a religion either.

MR. DOERR: You seem to think that there has not been any constitutional history on this. The Supreme Court, back in 1972 and 1973 and in subsequent decisions, examined several tuition tax credit programs from New York, Ohio, and New Jersey, and found them to be clearly unconstitutional. These programs were transferring money from the public treasury, for which we all are taxed, into the treasuries of religious institutions.

REPRESENTATIVE HYDE: With a tuition tax credit, Mr. Doerr, no money exchanges hands. The parent gets a deduction on his income tax.

MR. DOERR: That is not what the Supreme Court says.

REPRESENTATIVE HYDE: Those are the facts. You do not *give* money to anybody.

MR. DOERR: It is a fact that the public treasury goes down and the treasury of the parochial school goes up. It does not matter whether the dollar physically moved from one to the other.

REPRESENTATIVE HYDE: What about going to church on Sunday, putting a $20 bill in the collection box and then writing that off your income tax?

MR. DOERR: We all get deductions for contributions to religious and other charitable organizations, and that is provided across the board. But support for specifically religious institutions, the way tuition tax credits provide it, has been found by the Supreme Court to violate the Constitution.

REPRESENTATIVE HYDE: What is the essential constitutional difference between a deduction and a credit?

MR. LYNN: The essential constitutional difference is that the credit is closer to providing a direct subsidy to the institution and is worth much more.

MR. DOERR: There is a further infirmity. Tax aid, through tuition tax credits or vouchers or any other scheme, provides public support for the various kinds of invidious discrimination practiced by nonpublic schools—segregation according to creed, class discrimination, academic discrimination. There are a number of forms of discrimination that are practiced in nonpublic schools that would never be tolerated in public schools. Any form of federal or state aid to nonpublic schools means we are taxed to support those forms of discrimination.

REPRESENTATIVE HYDE: As long as the tax credit is allowed across the board to, for example, Methodist, Lutheran, Jewish, and Roman Catholic schools, it is my position that it is not unconstitutional. The second part of the First Amendment, which says that the free exercise of one's religion may not be prohibited, is violated by imposing a double burden on the parents who want to send their child to a parochial school.

MR. DOERR: By your logic, would you then support separate but equal schools for children of different races?

REPRESENTATIVE HYDE: Oh, no, no, not at all.

MR. DOERR: What's the difference between tax support for segregating kids by race and segregating them by religion?

REPRESENTATIVE HYDE: They are not segregated by religion. Every Roman Catholic parochial school in Chicago has a good percentage of non-Catholics and a mixture of races.

MR. DOERR: Oh, you can find some examples, but, nationwide, non-public schools approach 100 percent religious homogeneity. The Catholic schools are somewhat more mixed than some of the others.

REPRESENTATIVE HYDE: Your facts are wrong.

MR. DALY: Let's move to the battle being fought on the issues of science education. On the one hand, some legislators and educators around the country argue that evolution remains but one theory of man's beginning and that the Biblical account of creation is another. They therefore conclude that both theories should be taught as part of students' science education. On the other hand, the argument is made that evolution is science and that the teaching of Biblical creationism only serves to advance religion and should not be taught as science.

MR. LYNN: This is another nearly bogus issue, a phony equality of treatment. There is nothing similar between the scientific theory of evolution and the religious theory of creationism. Creationism probably should be taught in public schools, but it should be taught in a comparative religion class where it belongs. It should not be in the public schools masquerading as science.

Science begins with observation, goes to experimentation, then tries to find the truth or falsity of the hypothesis that it develops. Creationism starts with the conclusion that everything was created by God 10,000 years ago, and then seeks to find miscellaneous bits of information from a variety of sciences to support the conclusion. That is not science.

REPRESENTATIVE HYDE: That is like a decision made by the Supreme Court; the Court begins with a result and then looks for ways to justify it. An educated person ought to know about the theory of creation as well as evolution and others, and the theories ought to be presented to the kids in a nondiscriminatory way. The teacher can say, "I prefer this because this is scientific." This is a leap of faith. There are people who believe in creationism. I think one's education is incomplete if he does not understand that.

MR. LYNN: But you do not think it should be taught as science in the biology books of the United States.

REPRESENTATIVE HYDE: I do not think it is unscientific to say there are those who believe that a force created something out of nothing, because science does not yet give us an answer to the question of the "uncaused cause."

MR. LYNN: No, but neither do biology textbooks about evolution. They leave that first cause, the uncaused cause, out of biology books for a good reason.

REPRESENTATIVE HYDE: One can say, "now, take your science hat off and put your religion hat on; we're going to talk about creationism." But an educated person should know about both theories.

MR. DOERR: A teacher cannot take off his science hat and put on a religion hat. He has to be neutral.

REPRESENTATIVE HYDE: That is the sad thing for education.

MR. DOERR: Which religion hat would you have him put on in the school?

REPRESENTATIVE HYDE: All of the major religions: Islam, Judaism, Christianity—

MR. DOERR: This may be done now in social studies and comparative religion classes. I am a former social studies teacher. I talked about religious issues in an academically neutral way. This can be done. It is being done by thousands and thousands of teachers.

REPRESENTATIVE HYDE: I know, but when one is talking about creationism in science, one should not have to recess and go down the hall—

MR. LYNN: But do you want every religious doctrine to be taught that has something to do with explaining man's relationship to the universe?

REPRESENTATIVE HYDE: Just the major ones.

MR. LYNN: But just a few minutes ago, you said that we should not draw any distinctions about religion, that the Unification Church, the Baptist, the Methodist, the Catholic churches are all the same.

REPRESENTATIVE HYDE: You are talking about the time being spent teaching these things. I do not think there are that many theories about creationism. I do not think the Methodists and the Baptists have a different theory.

MR. LYNN: But there are not only Methodists and Baptists in the United States. There are, I think, 415 identifiable religious groups in this country today. There are hundreds of theories of Creation in the world.

MR. DOERR: The bottom line is that in a science class, the curriculum should be designed by scientists; in a Spanish class, it should be designed by experts in Spanish. Theologians should not be designing a curriculum just because they have an interest in a particular class.

MR. DALY: Let's move to the crèche decision by the Supreme Court if we may. Recently, the Court ruled, in the so-called *Pawtucket* case, that it is constitutional for a crèche to be included in a holiday display on public grounds. Does this decision bother any of you in this context of church-state relations?

MR. BERNS: The *Pawtucket* case is a beautiful example of why the ACLU should keep its nose out of public business. That was a case in which the ACLU filed a suit. The crèche was not on public property; it was purchased with public funds. The case ought to have been declared moot before it got to the Supreme Court of the United States because the city sold the crèche after it lost in the trial court, so there really was not any issue left.

Having said that nasty thing about the ACLU, let me try to defend it on more moderate grounds—defend my statement, that is to say, not the ACLU. The question ought to be raised as to why the Court granted standing in this particular case. As Mr. Lynn pointed out in the beginning, there are two parts to the First Amendment and, carried to extremes, the parts do, indeed, come into conflict with each other. To use my favorite example of this, we draft young men into the army and send them to remote places, and if we do not provide them with priests to administer the sacraments, we might be denying them the free exercise of their religion. But, when we employ the chaplain, we might be violating the law with respect to an establishment.

My point here is that many of these cases ought not to be litigated, and so I would ask the Court to ask the ACLU, "what skin off your nose is it that we have this crèche in Pawtucket?" By insisting on bringing this kind of a case to the Court, you might very well lose—as a matter of fact, you lost.

Now, what did you lose, and what have we lost because you lost that particular case? I would imagine that, in the past, many a city councilman, many a mayor has said, in effect, to some importunate constituent who asks for a religious display and so forth, "Charlie, you know doggone well we cannot do that. That gets into the First Amendment. The city cannot put crèches on top of the Palmolive building and so forth and so on." The consequence of the ACLU's pushing that suit and losing it is that it has deprived every mayor around the country of that response to all the Charlies, and there are lots of Charlies of lots of religions. Pretty soon the public world is going to be festooned with a variety of religious symbols.

MR. LYNN: One of the things that Justice Black said was that when you mix government and religion, you tend to destroy governments and degrade religion. In the *Pawtucket* case, we have the perfect example of the degradation of an important religious symbol because some "Charlie" in that state got his way with the mayor and the city council. Here, in fact, is the second-most-important symbol of the Christian faith—the manger scene, the baby Jesus—in the middle of clowns, a talking wishing-well, an elephant, a blue bear, some reindeer, and the Santa Claus house.

I cannot imagine anything more degrading to this central symbol of Christianity than that scene. I am surprised that someone did not come out in the middle of the night and destroy this scene in the Pawtucket Square, not because of his constitutional objections, but because he thought it blasphemous.

MR. BERNS: The consequence of the ACLU filing that suit, and the Court granting standing to the ACLU, is that we are going to see that important symbol of Christianity surrounded by red-nosed reindeer all over this broad land. Thank you very much, ACLU.

MR. LYNN: We already were seeing it. It is clear from this suit and other suits around the country that involve the mixing of religious symbols with secular symbols. There are parents who are deeply religious and deeply Christian who take the matter of Christmas seriously, and who try their darndest to keep the secular meaning of Christmas and Santa Claus separate from the historic and religious meaning of the birth of Jesus Christ.

MR. DALY: We have covered several of the major areas of conflict with respect to the Constitution and religion and have come to the question-and-answer session. May I have the first question, please?

AUSTIN RANNEY, resident scholar, American Enterprise Institute: I would like to ask a public policy question, and direct it to all the members of the panel. What makes you think that state support of religion in any form will do good, and what evidence do you have for that; equally, what makes you think that state support of religion will do harm, and what evidence do you have for that?

MR. BERNS: It was the opinion of George Washington, of course, uttered in his Farewell Address, that there is a connection between morality, to use our word, and the viability of our republican institutions. Further testimony is provided by Tocqueville, who developed this theme at great length, and indicated that the good health of the United States really did depend upon the continuation of certain habits. Tocqueville probably provides the most thematic treatment of this subject available to us. The question he discussed was how—under this Constitution, under democratic auspices, when everything points to individualism and taking care of one's self—are all of us, all citizens of the United States, reminded that we have some responsibility toward others? I would suppose that religious education does, in fact, somehow, go some way to remind us of that.

Whether school prayers conducted under the auspices of a typical member of the National Education Association performs that function, I have my doubts.

REPRESENTATIVE HYDE: I am inclined to agree with Mr. Berns. One is tempted to say religion might not help, but it certainly could not hurt to have an objective, non-discriminatory recognition of the fatherhood of God, if this agrees with a majority of people in a given community.

It is awfully hard to work on the brotherhood of man without some notion of the fatherhood of God—I, at least, have found it hard to prove the basic tenet, taken by itself, that all men are created equal. Clearly, human beings are different. There are smart ones and dumb ones, talented ones and klutzes. But if you do not consider the essentials, which are really God-given, you have problems proving our basic philosophy. What we need is an objective standard of morality, I think, rather than 235 million subjective standards of morality. So I, being very chary about abuses of the First Amendment and preferences of one religion over others, would like to see a return to the "fatherhood of God" notion.

MR. DOERR: Of course, there are many people of both genders who might feel that assigning a gender to God in that way is government taking a position on religion, and is therefore out of line.

REPRESENTATIVE HYDE: Oh, she does not mind. [Laughter.]

MR. DOERR: Okay, whatever. I think that Madison hit the nail on the head in his *Memorial and Remonstrance against Religious Assessments* in 1785, when he called attention to the fact that when government aids religion, it corrupts religion, it corrupts the clergy, it messes everything up. The evidence of history is that in those countries with a close union of church and state, where government subsidizes religion, promotes it, and tries to help it, there religion itself is corrupted and frequently becomes an ally of very bad politics.

In the American experience—I think Cardinal Cushing pointed this out—because we have implemented the principle of separation of church and state, we have had more religious tolerance and more religious freedom than any other society has ever known. When something ain't broke, as one of Murphy's corollaries has it, don't fix it. Church-state separation has been a great boon to our country. It is perhaps our most significant contribution to civilization. We should either leave it alone or try to enhance it.

MR. LYNN: Let me give you one very specific example of Mr. Doerr's point. In some schools in Michigan today, there is a program whereby public school teachers are paid to do part-time work by going into the parochial schools in Michigan and teaching subjects like advanced biology, music, and art appreciation, that would not otherwise be offered. But, in the process of sending those public school teachers into the private schools, in order to minimize the church-state conflict, all the religious pictures and the crucifixes are taken down from the walls of the classrooms that are used by those public school teachers. This takes what is sacred out of the school. The risk is that whenever one accepts benefits from Caesar, one may chip away a little piece of one's soul in the process.

Government support of religion tends to trivialize religion. That does not do any good for government and is bad for religion.

MR. BERNS: I should not like Mr. Doerr's response to remain as the final word on this question, "If it ain't broke, don't fix it." Let us not indulge the idea that the history of the United States is almost 200 unbroken years of complete separation of church and state. It certainly is not. There is more separation of church and state now than there was in the past. There certainly has been greater separation since the Supreme Court nationalized the First Amendment in 1947 and this whole issue became a national question. There certainly was more association of church and state on the state level, on the municipal level, in the past.

MR. DOERR: You are quite right, but I think we have been making progress, and it is to the good that we have greater separation now than we did 185 years ago.

REPRESENTATIVE HYDE: I am not satisfied that "it ain't broke," at least in terms of our society today. The narcotics problem is a tidal wave, whether we know it or not. We find it among athletes in sports and among all kinds of children in schools. As for pornography, we are so used to it now that it does not seem to do much—

MR. DOERR: What does that have to do with government meddling with religion?

REPRESENTATIVE HYDE: I am talking about how we have gotten away from such ideas as right and wrong, of God, of an objective standard of morality, and of sanctions against doing wrong or doing anything other than what the nerve endings say will be immediately gratifying.
    Society certainly is damaged, if not broken, and we should be looking for answers. A book on ethics isn't enough, in my opinion.

JUDE DOUGHERTY, dean of philosophy, the Catholic University of America: I have listened to the panel talk about religion as if the panel had, in fact, defined religion. Mr. Doerr speaks of religion as something very awful, whereas Representative Hyde speaks of religion in an altogether different sense. I wonder if we do not have to flesh out the meaning of the term before we can raise the question, Does the state have a stake in the practice of religion? Is there something that religion, considered as a community of worshippers, as a social structure, can deliver that perhaps no other unit within society can? The question is, specifically, What does the panel understand by religion, and isn't the quarrel really over who controls the education of children within the public school? Also, should there be one common school or a multiplicity of common schools?

MR. DOERR: I am a religious person and an active member of the board of my own church, so I do not deprecate religion in any way; I am very much involved in it. It is difficult in the time available to define religion; it comes in many shapes and forms. I define organized religion as people belonging to and working in associations called churches, congregations, or whatever. They mainly do good. But I think the good they do is independent of government, and there is nothing much government can do to enhance churches except let them alone.

As to whether we should have a multiplicity of schools funded by the government, an example of what can happen is Northern Ireland. There the children are segregated by religion from the time they are old enough to walk into school until the time they leave. As a result, there is incredible hatred and tension between the two main religious groups in Northern Ireland. That is an oversimplification, but it is very much applicable.

We have ever so much greater religious diversity in the United States. It would be national suicide, as James Conant said a generation ago, for us to subsidize the segregation of all American children along religious, ideological, or other lines. The pluralism we have is the pluralism of the public school, where kids and teachers of all faiths, racial backgrounds, and national backgrounds, rub together. The individual child does not run into very much pluralism in a nonpublic school where nearly all of his classmates and teachers are of the same faith and ideology as he.

REPRESENTATIVE HYDE: Most parochial schools are very pluralistic. I do not know what schools Mr. Doerr is acquainted with, but I am acquainted with many of them all over the country. One of my complaints is that they are much too secular rather than sectarian.

You picked Ireland, where the Catholics and the Protestants are at each other's throats. I would have thought you would have picked India, where the rioting going on is not so much economic as religious, or Iran and Iraq, where there are fundamentalist Moslems at each other's throats. Those cases are not the product of their religions; I do not think the religions of those people advocate such strife.

MR. DOERR: You don't think Khomeini's religion advocates intolerance? It certainly does.

REPRESENTATIVE HYDE: I think the fundamental books of the Moslem faith do not. I think it is a gentle faith, and I think what Khomeini is doing is a distortion of Islam.

MR. DOERR: If you would utter that opinion in Tehran, you would be in jail.

REPRESENTATIVE HYDE: Religion is from a Greek term that has to do with the bond between an individual and God. I define religion as the relationship of an individual to the Supreme Being, whether that is structured and organized or personal. That is religion, in my opinion, and I think it is indispensable to being an integrated person.

MR. DOERR: Benjamin Franklin said that if religion has to depend on government for support, that is a sign that it is a bad religion. A good religion can support itself without the help of government.

REPRESENTATIVE HYDE: Ben Franklin also asked that every session of the Constitutional Convention open with a prayer.

MR. DOERR: And his motion was not approved.

REPRESENTATIVE HYDE: Yes, because Hamilton and the others were concerned that people would think the delegates were not getting along very well if they had to open every day with prayer. [Laughter.] But as long as we open Congress with prayer, as long as the courts open with prayer, I do not see any problem with kids opening their school day with prayer.

MR. LYNN: Justice Rehnquist recently said some frightening things about America today. He suggested that religious divisiveness is not a real problem in twentieth-century America. But in the process of debate over such volatile issues as school prayer and equal access we have seen the most intense demagoguery to support governmental intrusions into religious matters. This demagoguery has surpassed the lobbying for all kinds of unpopular causes that I have experienced in my ten years in Washington. At no other time have I received the hate mail and the threats that I received simply because I think that government should be out of the prayer-writing and prayer-selecting business.

Many of the valiant and courageous members of the United States Senate, who debated the school prayer amendment on the floor, received letters that were as disgraceful to legitimate and honest political debate as any I have ever seen on any issue. I think the potential for religious divisiveness exists; it occurs in communities around this country when religious clubs begin to meet in high schools.

We see neighbors pitted against neighbors, children pitted against children; we even see homes burned down, homes belonging to those courageous people in communities that protest religious activities in the public schools. We are a hair's breadth away from true internecine, interreligious warfare in the United States. What we have seen happening in communities all over the country would certainly increase dramatically if we sent any constitutional amendment about church and state out for ratification by all the states.

MR. BERNS: I want to dissociate myself from what Mr. Lynn said, that we are a hair's breadth away from Khomeini's Iran or Ian Paisley's Northern Ireland, or Archbishop Laud's seventeenth-century Britain. I think that is hyperbole, to say the least.

I also want to say to Mr. Doerr that the issue is not about government supporting religion. The issue is, for example, whether tax exemption should be given to church property and so forth, and the Supreme Court has upheld that. That is the issue, not whether we have an established church in the full sense of the term. No one on this panel wants an established church in the United States. Everybody on this panel is in favor of toleration. Everyone on this panel would abhor the situation that Mr. Lynn described and certainly would not take any action leading to such a situation.

A.E. DICK HOWARD, professor of law and public affairs, University of Virginia: The panel has made clear the role of the Supreme Court, especially since 1947, in importing the notion of the "wall of separation" into its First Amendment decisions on religion. In light of that, it is rather striking that the three most recent significant Supreme Court decisions have all been, in effect, accommodations; they have all upheld challenged state measures. The Minnesota case upheld tuition tax credits, the Nebraska case upheld the paying of chaplains, and the Pawtucket, Rhode Island, case upheld the display of the crèche. Do those three cases simply represent some marginal adjustment in the Court's thinking about the First Amendment, or are we now, all these years after *Everson*, seeing something that may portend a major adjustment toward more accommodation by states, and by government generally, to religious practices in the public arena?

MR. LYNN: I would not call what has happened simple accommodation, because there is lengthy, serious, and thoughtful case law about accommodating religious beliefs. At what point can one exempt individuals, on religious grounds, from laws of general applicability? The decisions you mentioned have gone much further than that. They are not accommodations; they come dangerously close to what we mean by establishment. The very absence of neutrality creates the dangers of which I spoke—that is, the degrading of religion, the trivializing of religion, and the creation of political warfare among religious groups.

I think these have been bad decisions. Most of them, thankfully, are very narrow decisions. It will depend, to some degree, on the quality and the capabilities of the next few appointees to the Supreme Court as to whether we will see a trend toward establishment instead of a responsible recognition of accommodation.

REPRESENTATIVE HYDE: I disagree. They are fine decisions. The absolute nature of the *Everson* decision is being recognized as not having been based on scholarship. That case was not based on how the First Congress and the framers felt and acted, or on how the early presidents felt and acted, but was based on what the Court felt the law ought to be at that time.

Whether these recent cases represent a significant shift in the Court's thinking will depend on the personnel of the Court, and that is the vice of letting the Court write legislation or rewrite the Constitution according to their prepossessions.

It is interesting that, about the turn of the century, the Court was anathema to the progressive forces of America because it was reactionary. Today, or recently, when it has been a liberal court, it has been the darling of the progressive forces, and the Congress, the elected body, is anathema.

ERVIN S. DUGGAN, Ervin S. Duggan & Associates: My question is for Mr. Doerr, and has to do with the idea of a civil religion. Would you tell us what you meant by that, and perhaps the other members of the panel can comment on what they think about the idea of a civil religion in America.

MR. DOERR: I wish I could. It is not that easy. Robert Bellah and others have written on this concept of a civil religion for a number of years now, and it has to do with a patriotic type of common piety that is not pinned to any specific doctrine. Many deeply religious people think that this sort of civil religion makes a mockery of true religion and is too easily used by politicians to distract attention from the country's real problems. I am afraid that I have not seen the concept of civil religion precisely defined.

MR. BERNS: Strictly speaking, a civil religion would be a religion recognized by the city, if you will, and the subject, of course, has been treated by people like Rousseau.

ELIZABETH LITTLE, Concerned Women for America: Mr. Lynn, you stated that you are against any doctrinal instruction of children. Many parents extremely dislike their children being taught situation ethics in school with public tax money. These parents believe that there are intrinsic rights and instrinsic wrongs, and they find this philosophy of situation ethics quite in conflict with their moral standards. What rights do you think these parents have?

MR. LYNN: Parents have a right to expect that, in a class dealing with questions of values, students will be taught that some people believe there are different values depending on the situations, and other people believe there are fundamental and correct positions of right and wrong on the great moral questions of the day. Any school not teaching that both of these views are responsible ways to do moral analysis is a school that needs a little help and whose teachers need a little help. But I resist the idea that seems implicit in your question that somehow situation ethics has been prescribed as the national or state religion, or that secular humanism or some other phrase reflecting a point of view about values has been established as the national religion. It has not. None of this has happened. Courses in ethics and in processes of moral reasoning are appropriate in the schools and should reflect the many, many dozens of varieties of ethical thinking.

MR. BERNS: I am a member of the National Council of the Humanities, and the question of support from federal tax dollars comes up quite frequently regarding situation ethics or some variety of it, and the teaching of such at the seventh-grade level, for example. I would prefer to have children at that level told, with some authority behind it, that it is wrong to murder another human being or to steal from that other human being, et cetera, than to have these subjects introduced as debatable propositions, and I think this is a fair way of stating it. If we are concerned, as the Supreme Court is, about the difference between older and younger students, and about what might be done in colleges with older people and not done with younger children because younger children are more impressionable, I think that carries over here, too. I want to impress on young people that murdering other human beings is not debatable.

MR. LYNN: When you get beyond those two examples —murdering and stealing—what is the basis for the moral absolutes you would teach?

MR. BERNS: I absolutely recognize the problem you are getting at. We have to avoid anything that leads us in the direction of Ian Paisley or the Ayatollah Khomeini. I do not minimize the problem at all, Mr. Lynn.

MR. DOERR: Of course, teaching values in school is not a simple matter of one, two, three, this is the truth, and it cannot be questioned. I think teachers have a more sophisticated approach to the situation. You do not say a murder is wrong simply because I say so or because it is in the Ten Commandments. It is appropriate for a teacher to encourage a class of kids to discuss why a murder is wrong, why stealing is wrong, and—

MR. BERNS: You can try that with me, Mr. Doerr, and I can figure out some reasons why those things are not wrong; I suspect a ten-year-old can too.

REPRESENTATIVE HYDE: I just spent some time with Senator Jeremiah Denton of Alabama after having read his book *When Hell Was in Session*. He spent seven-and-a-half years in a prison camp in North Vietnam, four of those years in solitary confinement. And I got from that book the fact that he would never have survived without a strong religious faith.

That does not cut one way or the other in our discussion except to say that his religious faith proved valuable. Situation ethics would not have helped him survive while he was in solitary confinement or being tortured. His religious faith did. I note that the military academies compel attendance at religious services if you belong to a given religion.

MR. DOERR: No, they do not. The federal court of appeals in Washington several years ago ruled that the service academies cannot compel students to attend worship.

REPRESENTATIVE HYDE: We disagree.

MR. LYNN: I believe it is wrong to say that one cannot have a strong religious faith and still believe in situation ethics. There is great debate among Christians as to whether Jesus himself was a situationalist.

REPRESENTATIVE HYDE: Cardinal Newman asked, "Who was ever consoled in time of real trouble by the small beer of literature and music?" and I am just suggesting a strong religious faith can save your life sometimes.

30

MAURY ABRAHAM, Unitarian Universalist Association: I would like to ask the panelists to comment on the recent appointment of a U.S. ambassador to the Holy See.

REPRESENTATIVE HYDE: I do not think it is any big deal, frankly; it is a change in title. I know it offended many people who think the naming of an ambassador to a religion is a violation of separation of church and state. I do not know if it was worth all of the fuss that it created; I do not think it is an earth-shaking event.

MR. LYNN: It certainly gives added credibility to the notion that one religion is favored—the Roman Catholic faith—because we do not have an ambassador going to the World Council of Churches in Geneva, Switzerland, serving as a representative of the United States.

REPRESENTATIVE HYDE: I would vote for that if we did.

MR. LYNN: Would you? Even the World Council of Churches?

REPRESENTATIVE HYDE: Sure.

MR. LYNN: The appointment of the ambassador also gives a favored status to the Roman Catholic church because this makes it much easier for that religious organization to speak to the United States government through the Department of State. It gives them access that is not given to any other faith in the United States.

REPRESENTATIVE HYDE: Do you mean the apostolic delegate, now that he is an ambassador, will make any difference at all?

MR. LYNN: He may, and I think another problem is created for American Catholics. I wonder if this will not lead U.S. officials to inappropriate meddling with papal representatives to influence policy being made by the American bishops. That also worries me.

MR. DOERR: Another matter that concerns many Catholics is the fact that part of the justification for naming an ambassador to the Holy See is that it would enable the U.S. government to tap the intelligence network that the Catholic church allegedly has. What this tells revolutionaries, the Shining Path movement in Peru, for instance, is that from now on Catholic priests, missionaries, and nuns may be spying for the CIA, and they may become fair targets. This establishment of relations with the Holy See may actually endanger the lives of Catholic missionaries working in the third world, according to some Catholics.

MR. BERNS: I doubt whether the appointment of this ambassador makes the Roman Catholic church the established church of the United States. In fact, we already have an established church in the United States; it's the Old Order Amish, because the Old Order Amish are entitled, as no other group is, to disobey a law that is a valid criminal statute, thanks to the Supreme Court of the United States in *Wisconsin* v. *Yoder.*

The interesting thing is that in the name of the Free Exercise Clause, the Court has gone to astonishing lengths. Freedom of religion manifests itself in our time as demands for exemption from laws applying to everyone. That is what Yoder did. He is an Old Order Amish man who refused to send his child—probably with good reason—to the local public high school. [Laughter.] There was a criminal statute under which he was fined $5.00, I think—talk about small beer—and the Supreme Court allowed this to come before it and ruled in Yoder's favor because he was Old Order Amish. The Court then went on to say that this did not hold for any other group, just Old Order Amish. That is the established church in the United States, Old Order Amish.

MR. LYNN: If you do not think that is a legitimate free exercise issue, then what possible meaning does the Free Exercise Clause have?

MR. BERNS: Jefferson gave us the formula for that.

MR. LYNN: If one cannot be exempted from laws because of religious belief, what else is there to the Free Exercise Clause?

MR. BERNS: It is a fundamental principle of American government that no one, because of his religious faith, shall be exempted from the necessity to obey valid criminal statutes; once you start down the road of exemption, there will be a proliferation of sects in this country, given the opposition of churches to paying taxes and all.

MR. LYNN: A compelling government interest has been raised in those cases, and we have not seen the floodgates open to every cult, sect, and faith in America because of the Old Order Amish. We have a very responsible decision that puts some meat into the Free Exercise Clause; some of us believe that the meat is necessary in both the Establishment Clause and the Free Exercise Clause.

REPRESENTATIVE HYDE: Didn't Timothy Leary try to start the League for Spiritual Development, and didn't that involve the use of LSD? The courts did not uphold that.

MR. LYNN: But the courts have upheld the use of peyote by the Native American church because such use is central to the very religious beliefs of that organization.

MR. BERNS: Jefferson's formula covered this. It is no denial of the Free Exercise Clause; one can pray and so forth, but one must obey the law. That's it. We cannot afford to take the route that allows someone to exempt himself. If I could refuse, as a Marine, to go to Lebanon because I refuse to shoot my Muslim brothers there, what sort of an army would we have? Or, to be precise, what sort of Marine Corps would we have if that sort of thing is allowed, Mr. Lynn? No thank you.

MR. LYNN: Do you want the man who does not want to fight and who will not kill his Muslim brethren to be in Lebanon next to you in the foxhole? I suspect you do not.

MR. BERNS: I do not, but I would prefer that that exemption be established by congressional statute. Somebody in the Marine Corps who does not want to go fight where the Marine Corps has to fight ought not to be in the Marine Corps.

MR. LYNN: He should be discharged. This kind of incident just occurred, and discharge was sought.

MR. BERNS: Mr. Lynn, is the ACLU going to litigate that case?

MR. LYNN: We are not, to my knowledge, involved in that specific case, but we have been involved in cases for the past fifty years on the question of conscientious objection to military service. As you know, it is a very lively issue yet today because the Congress has failed to provide the opportunity in the current draft registration system for conscientious objectors to indicate that they are conscientious objectors and do not wish to be considered a part of that pool of persons eligible, willing, and able to go to fight whenever their government calls them.

REPRESENTATIVE HYDE: But you know they will have an opportunity to declare their conscientious objection if and whenever we reestablish the draft, which may or may not happen.

MR. LYNN: —If the Congress decides to preserve that right, which the courts have said is just a matter of legislative grace.

MR. DALY: This concludes another public policy forum presented by the American Enterprise Institute for Public Policy Research. On behalf of AEI, our hearty thanks to our distinguished and expert panelists, Mr. Walter Berns, Representative Henry J. Hyde, Mr. Edd Doerr, and the Reverend Barry Lynn, and also our thanks to our guests and experts in the audience for their participation.

The AEI Project, "A Decade of Study of the Constitution," of which publication of this Public Policy Forum transcript is one activity, has been funded in part by a grant from the National Endowment for the Humanities.

www.ingramcontent.com/pod-product-compliance
Lightning Source LLC
Jackson TN
JSHW011409130125
77033JS00023B/929